Humble, Richard

The age of Leif Eriksson

EXPLORATION THROUGH THE AGES

THE AGE OF LEIF ERIKSSON

Richard Humble

Illustrated by
Richard Hook

Franklin Watts
New York · London · Toronto · Sydney

First published in the United States by
Franklin Watts Inc.
387 Park Avenue South
New York, NY 10016

Library of Congress Cataloging-in-Publication Data

Humble, Richard.
The age of Leif Eriksson/by Richard Humble.
p. cm. – (Exploration through the ages)
Includes index.
Summary: Chronicles the Vikings' exploration and colonization of Greenland, Iceland, and North America.
ISBN 0-531-10741-8
1. Leiv Eiriksson, d. ca. 1020 — Juvenile literature.
2. Explorers – Norway – Biography – Juvenile literature. 3. Explorers – America Biography Juvenile literature. 1. America – Discovery and exploration – Norse – Juvenile literature.
[1. Vikings. 2. America – Discovery and exploration – Norse.] I. Title II. Series.
E105.L47H86 1989
970.01'3–dc20 89-8867
CIP
AC

Designer: Ben White
Illustrations: Richard Hook,
Jim Robins, Hayward Art Group

Photographs: Courtesy of Canada House, p.29

Printed in Belgium

Words in bold appear in the glossary

Contents

"West over seas"

The Vikings of Denmark, Norway and Sweden were the terror of Europe for over 200 years. From about AD 790 to 1050, raiding armies of Viking warriors killed and robbed wherever their fleets of longships could float.

But the Vikings were far more than just a race of seagoing fighting thieves. They were also great farmers, traders, artists, and, above all, great explorers and settlers. They had a restless urge to find new lands in which to live in freedom – an urge that carried them further and further "west over seas," as their heroic poems or **sagas** put it.

By the second half of the ninth century, 850–900, Viking settlers were well established in northern and eastern England, along the east coast of Ireland, in the Isle of Man, the Hebrides, the Orkneys, and the Shetland Islands. Viking explorers from Norway had also settled in the Faroe Islands, 684 km (425 miles) out in the Atlantic Ocean.

By Viking tradition, Iceland, only 450 km (280 miles) northwest of the Faroes, was first sighted by two sailors on two different voyages – Gardar of Sweden and Naddod of Faroe – who were blown far off course by Atlantic storms. The position of Iceland, a big and empty land ripe for settlement, was well known to the Vikings by the year 870.

Between 890 and 930, about 20,000 Norwegians – men, women and children, with their farm animals – had sailed via the Shetlands and Faroes to start a new life in Iceland. The new colony flourished. It had its own laws and parliament known as the **Althing**.

It was from Iceland that Viking exploration was continued in the late 900s striking out even further "west over seas."

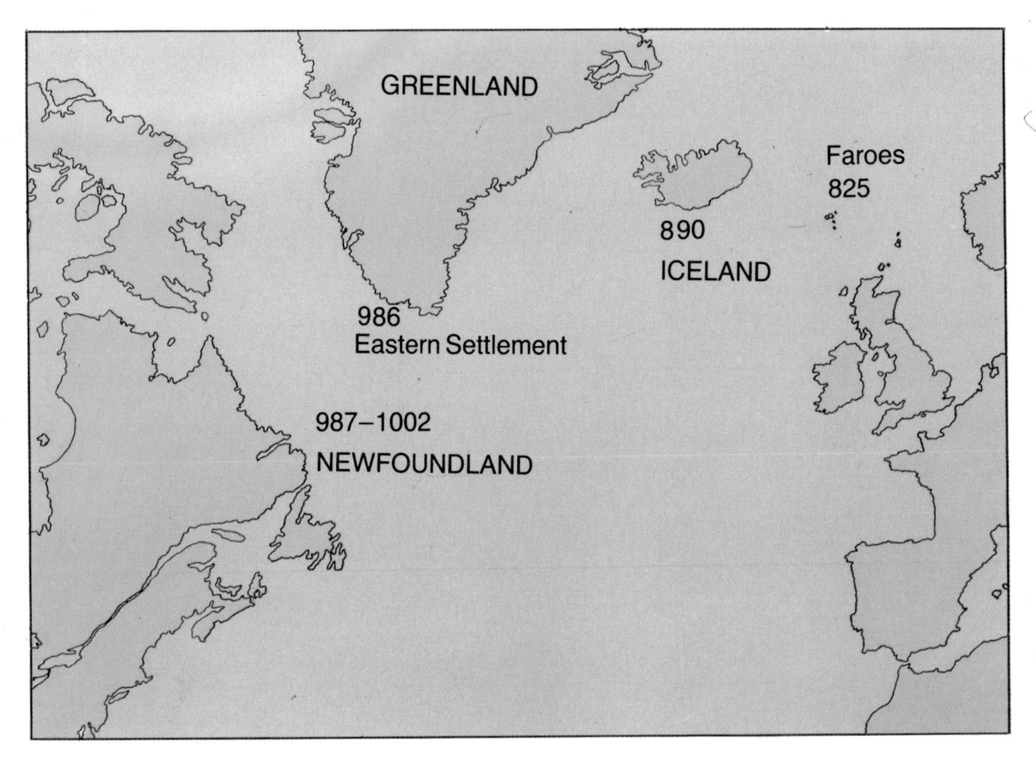

◁ The main ocean routes taken by Viking seamen probing "west over seas," with dates of settlement. By 950 the long sea route from Norway to Iceland, via the Shetland and Faroe Islands, was well known to experienced seafarers.

▷ A Viking family sailing to start a new life in Iceland copes with rough weather in the Atlantic, bailing out water and hauling covers over the supplies and household goods lashed down **amidships**. For women and children, this was the only shelter out at sea.

The Viking longship

Viking warships were long and narrow, built for speed when sailing under oar and sail. But the longships that carried Viking explorers, settlers and traders across the Atlantic were different.

Where the Viking warship was designed to hold the maximum number of fighting men, on at least 20 oar benches, the Viking trading ships were designed to carry maximum cargo. Compared with the warships they were shorter, broader, and had higher sides, or **bulwarks**, which kept out the sea and enabled more cargo and livestock to be stored amidships.

△ At the start of an ocean voyage, a fully-loaded knorr heads out to sea under oars as crewmen hoist the square sail.

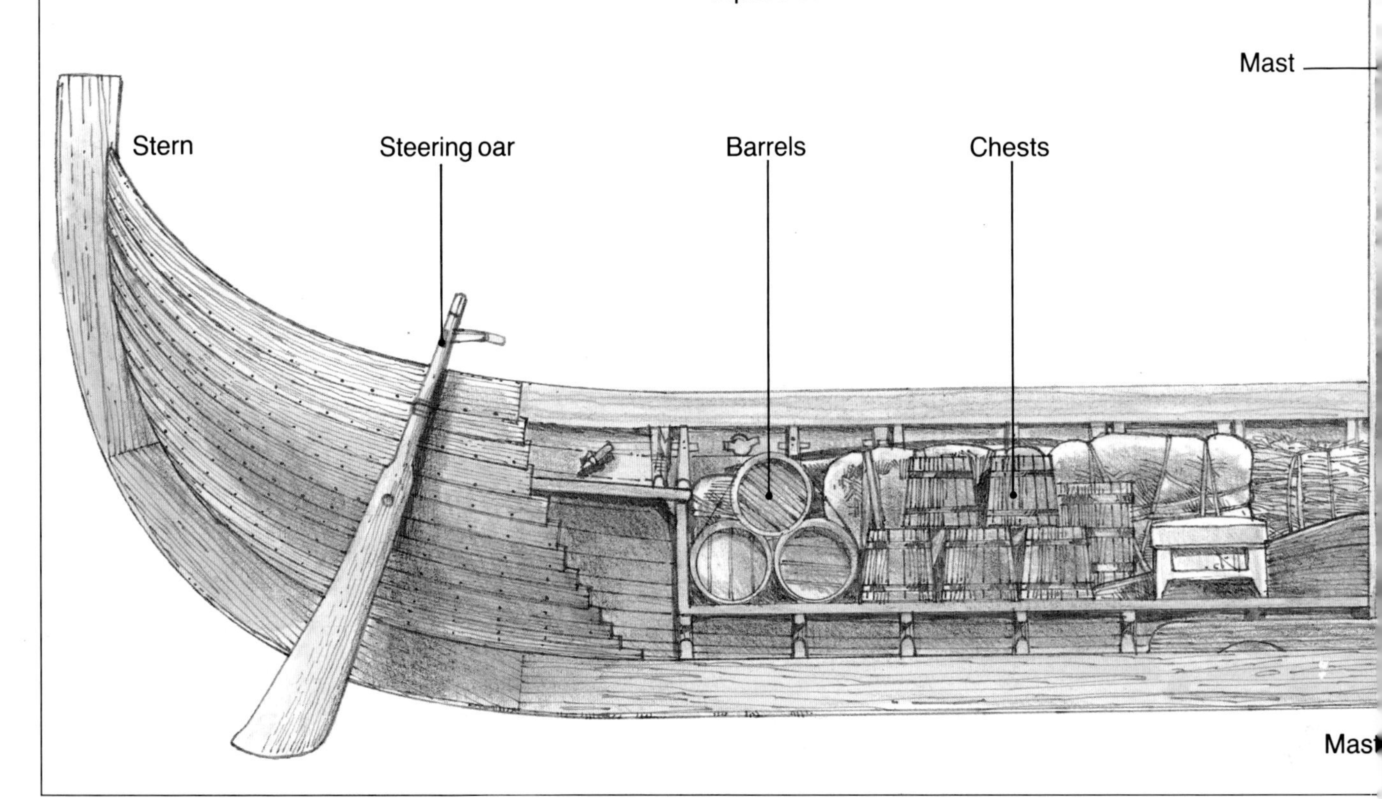

△ Beached in the shallows, a knorr is heeled over to help her crew unload stores and livestock over the side and on to the beach.

Where the Vikings used names like **drekar** ("dragon") to distinguish their warships, the word most used for sea-going trading ships was **knorr**.

The knorr shared the same basic features as the fighting drekar. It had the same **clinker-built** construction of overlapping planks. It had a keel, to enable the ship to be sailed close to the wind. It was steered by a broad-bladed oar on the **starboard** side of the ship, and it had the same type of woven square sail, reinforced with a checkerboard pattern of leather strips.

The knorr also used oars when putting out to sea or heading into shallow waters, and it could be beached and heeled over for the landing of cargo.

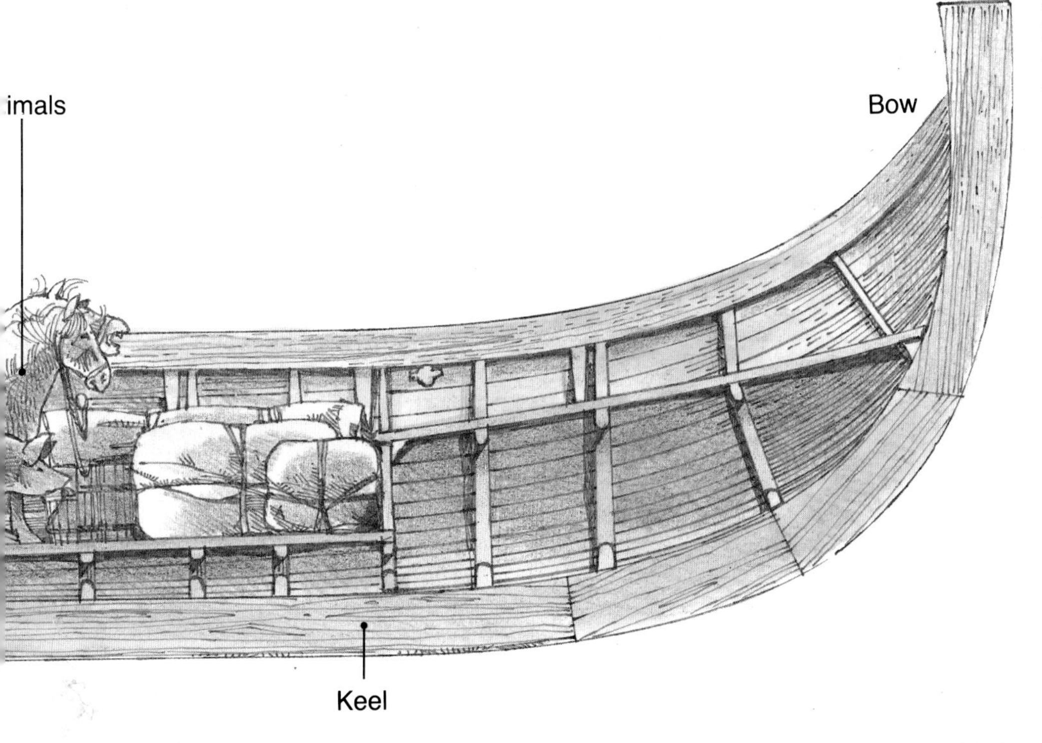

◁ Though no complete knorrs have been recovered yet, this is probably what these ships looked like. Basic construction resembled that of the longer, sleeker warships, with a shell of overlapping planks held together inside by cross-frames supporting a deck. A long supporting **step** spread the weight and stress of the single mast. Stores and livestock were stacked and tied down amidships. Covers could be stretched over a framework to protect the stores in rough weather.

Seamanship

Viking ships were wonderfully seaworthy. The hulls of the ships needed to be flexible to "give" against the pounding of high seas. The ability of these ships to make long ocean voyages was proved in 1893 when a replica of a Viking warship crossed the Atlantic.

Viking sailors were highly skilled at getting maximum performance out of the single square sail. Though this was naturally most effective with the wind astern, it could be braced with a long spar for tacking against the wind.

◁ The magnetic compass was unknown to the Vikings, but they understood that a ship's latitude (north/south position) could be measured by the height of the sun or North Star above the horizon. Their likeliest instrument was the **pelorus**. (*above*)

▽ A knorr at sea, sailing close-hauled to the wind, whose direction is shown by the windvane at the top of the mast.

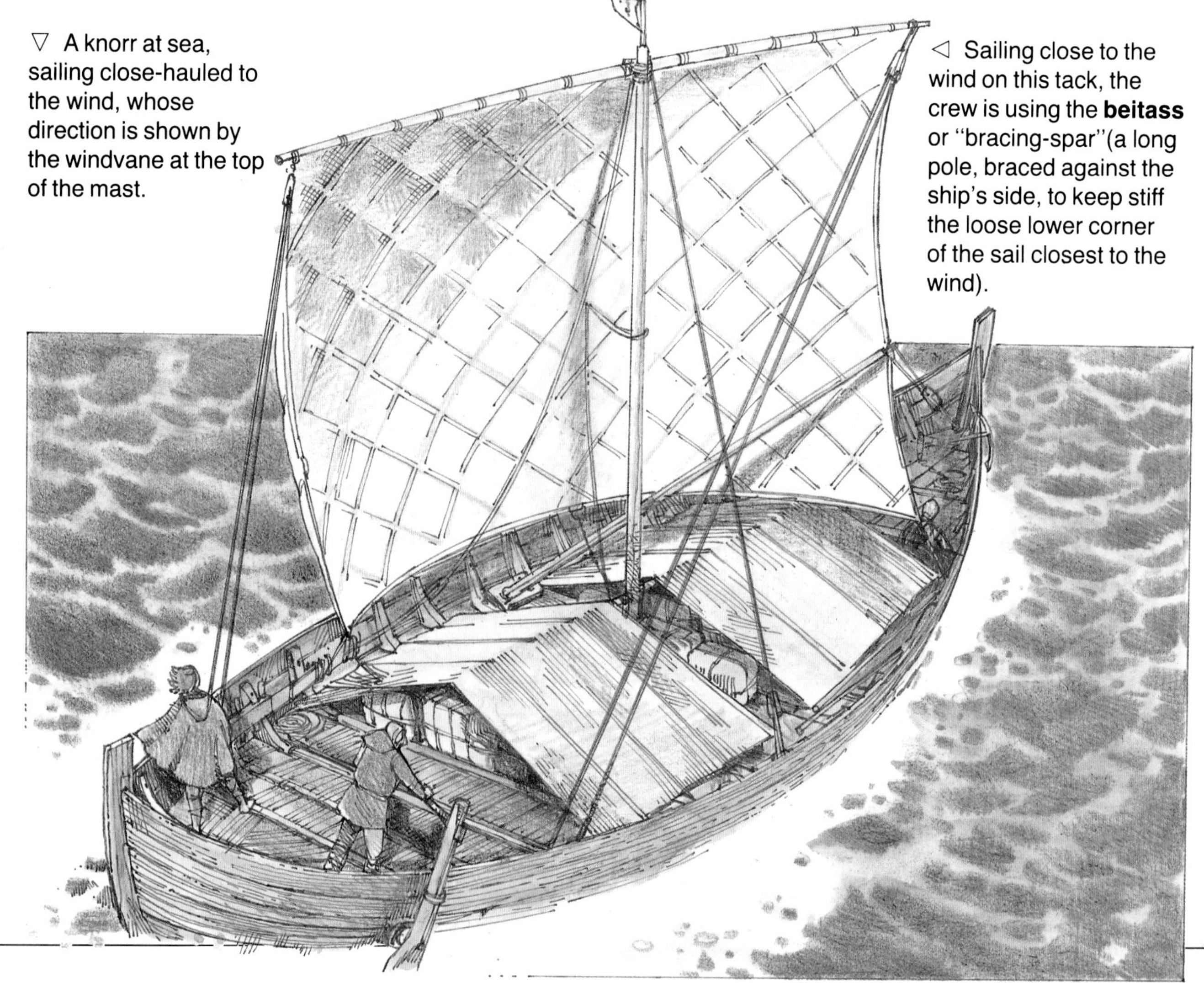

◁ Sailing close to the wind on this tack, the crew is using the **beitass** or "bracing-spar"(a long pole, braced against the ship's side, to keep stiff the loose lower corner of the sail closest to the wind).

Life on a Viking ship during a long sea voyage was not for the weak or faint-hearted – it could be endlessly cold. However, most voyages consisted of relatively short passages between well-known landmarks – except when storms blew the ship off course. When this happened, all the navigating skills of the captain were needed in order to reach land before the crew's limited water supplies ran out. In Viking tradition, it was during such delays that most new lands, like Iceland and Greenland, were discovered.

△ Sleeping bags helped keep out the night wind, while wet woolen clothing provided good insulation from the cold.

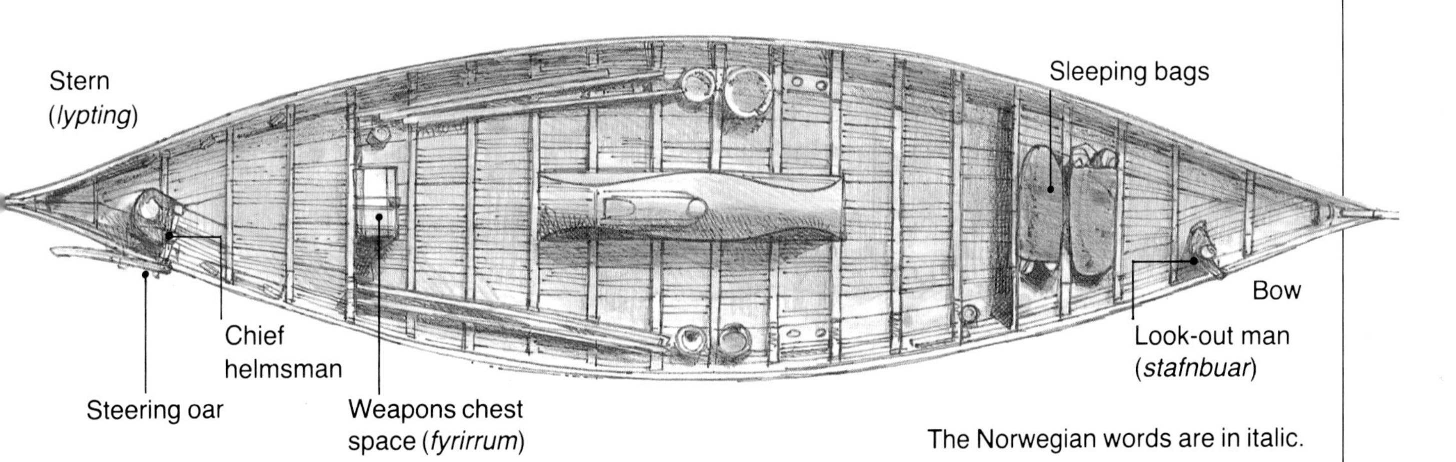

The Norwegian words are in italic.

Through the ages, one of the greatest dangers to sailors has been exhaustion made worse by hunger, thirst and cold. In order to preserve their food, Vikings salted it. They also ate fish and gulls which they caught at sea. Sleeping bags and limited shelter meant that most voyages were wet ones, but layers of woolen clothing helped keep out the cold.

△ Though no two voyages, cargoes or crews were identical, this shows the basic crew and cargo area.

▷ There were no cooking fires on board. Salted fish and bacon were the usual preserved foods, supplemented by fresh fish and seagulls.

At Aegir's mercy

Excellent sailors though they were, the Vikings were not supermen. They were tough professionals with a healthy respect for the sea and the fierceness of its often changing weather. It was not surprising that one of the most important Viking gods was **Aegir**, god of the sea and its storms. To Aegir every sailor entrusted his life and the safety of his goods whenever he went out to sea.

The perils of the sea are an essential part of the Viking story. Many fleets of raiding ships were caught by storms and smashed on unfamiliar coasts.

An Irish poem of the Viking era rejoiced in the bad weather at sea, for then Western folk were safe: "fierce Northmen only course the quiet seas."

Viking sagas tell of how the first colonists came to Iceland. The man who led the first fleet of settlers to Iceland, Ingolf Arnarsson, threw some of his furniture into the sea. He vowed to found his settlement wherever Aegir might cast them ashore; this was at what is now the modern city of Reykjavik in Iceland. But Ingolf's people had barely established themselves there when, around the year 900, a gale drove Gunnbjörn Ulfsson's ship past Iceland to a new land in the west. This was the barren coast of Greenland.

◁ On the now-routine trading run from the Faroes to Iceland, an Atlantic storm drives a Viking merchant ship before the gale. As the cargo and livestock are hastily lashed down, a crate of chickens is hurled over the side as a sacrifice to calm the wrath of Aegir.

Erik lands in Greenland

Many Viking explorers chose to voyage "west over seas" simply because times were changing at home. Laws in the well-ordered kingdom of Norway were too strict for many men. Ingolf Arnarsson, the first major settler of Iceland, was exiled from Norway because he committed the crime of murder. Thorvald Asvaldson and his son, Erik the Red, were also exiled in 981–82. Erik had already been exiled from Norway and after repeated feuding with his neighbors in western Iceland, he was exiled from Iceland too. As an outlaw, he decided to explore the unknown land sighted by Gunnbjörn 80 years before.

Erik made no attempt to land where he first approached the coast of the new land, for here was the massive Ingolfsfjeld Glacier, which was 1,830m (6,000 ft)

high. Instead, he sailed southward down the coast. He rounded what is know today as Cape Farewell, and landed on what became known as "Erik's Island" situated off the less forbidding west coast of what was clearly an enormous new country.

Once ashore, Erik told his crew that they would spend the winter there – always a sure sign that Vikings had come to stake a firm claim on new territory. It must have been a rough winter, living in leather tents and sod huts, with seal meat and blubber for food, heat and lighting. But in the spring Erik and his crew were on the move again, delighted by the spring grass growing beneath the towering glaciers further inland. That summer Erik explored the wilderness to the west and gave names to many landmarks there. After spending the second winter in the new land and the third on Erik's Island, Erik sailed for Iceland.

He was still an exile according to Icelandic law, and he had no intention of returning for good. He was determined to persuade as many Icelanders as he could to sail with him to the new land, where they would found a new Viking colony under Erik's rule.

Erik decided not to mention the ice mountains he had seen. He cleverly referred to the forbidding landscape of Iceland, and he stressed the fact that the land he had visited lay south of Iceland.

"He named the country he had discovered Greenland," says the **Greenland Saga**, "for he said that people would be more tempted to go there if it had an attractive name". In the year of 986, he sailed for Greenland with a fleet of 25 ships.

◁ Erik the Red's crew prepares for its first winter in the new land–Erik's Island. As supplies are unloaded and the first leather tent is pitched, the Icelanders look around to assess their new home. The most encouraging fact is that the waters teem with fish, and seals that can provide them with food, blubber and skins.

The Greenland colony

According to the *Saga*, only 14 of the original 25 ships that sailed with Erik made it to Greenland. "Some were driven back, and some were lost at sea." Allowing for the fact that 20 passengers sailed with each ship, this means that at least 250 colonists landed in Greenland – far more than the 101 Pilgrim Fathers who sailed for America from England in the *Mayflower* in 1620.

Looking back across a thousand years, it is easy to imagine the feelings of Erik's followers when they landed and took stock of their new land. Those who had found life tough in Iceland must have been horrified at their first sight of Greenland. Despite the welcoming green grass on the coast, the cold breath of Greenland's massive ice-cap – unknown in Iceland – must have caused a chill in their hearts.

Even a strong leader like Erik could not have prevented his followers from heading home if they had insisted, for the power of every free man's vote was strong in Viking society. Yet there is no record of any protest, mutiny or demand to return to Iceland. This shows how keen the Vikings were to settle and make a new life in even the most hostile and forbidding lands.

Nine leaders were content to settle near what became known as "Erik's **Fjord**."

◁ Life in Greenland's Eastern Settlement around the year 990. In the foreground, a craftsman slices walrus hide to prepare it for weaving into rope; on the shore of the fjord, another harpooned walrus is killed for its hide, blubber, and the "sea ivory" of its tusks.

Here, Erik's farm at Brattahlid (Steep Slope) became the capital of the new colony. Other colonists, who sought freedom from Erik's rule, headed 322 km (200 miles) up Greenland's west coast to found what soon became known as the **Western Settlement**. Erik's larger group of homesteads, further to the southeast, was called the **Eastern Settlement**.

Unlike Iceland, Greenland is not washed by the warm waters of the Gulf Stream, but histories of the colony show that Greenland was much warmer 1,000 years ago. The Greenlanders had quite enough summer grassland on which to raise sheep, cattle, pigs, goats and ponies. The fjords were alive with fish, and there was game hunting for reindeer, seals, walruses, whales and polar bears.

The Greenlanders lived in stone huts thatched with pieces of turf; their fuel came from turf peat and seal and whale blubber. They brought their furniture from Iceland and Norway – carved wooden benches and beds, stools, tables, cooking utensils and tools. This furniture was handed down from generation to generation.

The colonists' three greatest needs were wood, corn and iron, brought in by regular voyages from Iceland and Norway. For these necessities the Greenlanders were able to trade luxury goods: prized polar bear pelts and sealskins, ivory from walrus tusks, tough ropes woven from walrus skins, and the spiral tusks of the **narwhal** or "sea unicorn," prized throughout the known world for their supposed magical qualities.

New land to the west

Before Erik's colony on Greenland was six months old, another Viking voyage strayed off course and discovered strange lands even further to the west.

Bjarni Herjolfsson was the son of Herjolf Bardarson of Iceland, one of the nine leaders named in the *Greenland Saga* who sailed with Erik the Red and founded the Eastern Settlement.

"Bjarni", says the *Saga*, "was a man of much promise. From early youth he had been eager to sail to foreign lands; he earned himself both wealth and a good reputation, and used to spend his winters alternately abroad and in Iceland with his father."

In the summer when Erik's expedition sailed for Greenland, Bjarni set off for Iceland from Norway, not knowing that his father had decided to emigrate with Erik. When he reached Iceland he found that his father had sailed for Greenland, so Bjarni persuaded his crew to follow, frankly admitting the risk: "This voyage of ours will be considered foolhardy, for not one of us has ever sailed the Greenland Sea."

And so it proved. Three days out from Iceland, Bjarni's ship ran into fogs and northerly winds. Several days passed before they sighted the sun again and were able to get their bearings.

▽ Inuit carvings of human figures in cloaks and hoods. These were costumes similar to those worn by Vikings.

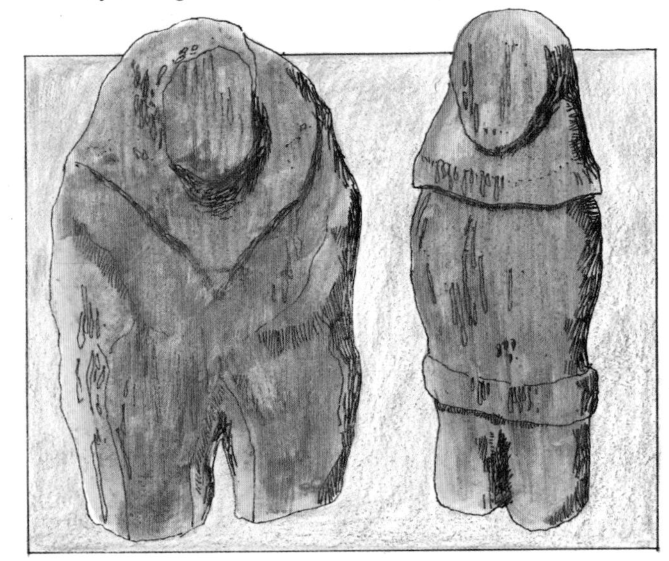

▷ Sailing north in their search for Greenland, Bjarni's crew gaze in wonder at the new land they sight to the west.

After a day's sailing, they sighted land: low-lying, with wooded hills. Bjarni was confident that this was not Greenland and sailed north for two days before sighting land again, which was also flat and wooded. This, too, Bjarni knew could not be Greenland, as there were said to be huge glaciers there.

Bjarni now headed out to sea and sailed for three days before sighting a third land. This one was high and mountainous and topped by a glacier. However, it turned out to be an island, and Bjarni headed out to sea yet again. After sailing before a gale for four days, a fourth land was sighted – and this time Bjarni was satisfied. "This tallies most closely with what I have been told about Greenland," he said, and headed for shore to land precisely at his father Herjolf's farm. News of the new lands caused great excitement in Greenland.

Leif Eriksson sails

Bjarni Herjolfsson was a strange character. When he landed in Greenland after his voyage of discovery to the west, he "gave up trading and stayed with his father, and carried on farming there after his father's death." For this he was blamed by the excited Greenlanders. "People thought he had shown great lack of curiosity, since he could tell them nothing about these countries."

One man was determined to follow where Bjarni had accidentally led the way. This was Erik the Red's son Leif, who went to see Bjarni, bought his ship, and had no trouble raising a crew of 35 men with whom to sail to the strange lands which Bjarni had sighted.

Leif asked his father to lead the expedition, urging the old warrior that under his command the voyage would have more good fortune than if commanded by any of his kinsmen. Erik was not eager; he protested that he was getting old and was no longer fit enough

to endure the hardships of sea voyaging. However, in the end he agreed.

As Erik and Leif were riding down to where the ship and its crew lay waiting at the fjord's edge, Erik's horse stumbled and threw him, injuring his leg. Such an accident was considered by Viking superstition to be the worst of omens for a journey. "I am not meant to discover more countries than this one we now live in," insisted Erik. "This is as far as we go together."

But the warning of bad luck that sent Erik the Red back to his home at Brattahlid did not stop either Leif or the waiting crew. Leif went straight abroad and gave the order to sail – and the first planned attempt by Europeans to sail to what is now known as the American mainland got under way.

Nothing says more about the confidence of Viking sailors than this voyage of Leif Eriksson, which left Greenland in the summer of 986 or 987. Just as Bjarni Herjolfsson had set sail for Greenland knowing nothing about the place apart from what he had learned in Iceland, so Leif Eriksson – with no more information about the lands in the west than what Bjarni had told him – now set out to retrace Bjarni's voyage, but in the reverse direction.

◁ With his ship and crew ready to sail, Leif hears his father, Erik, refuse to take command of the voyage, pleading ill luck after falling from his horse. On the left a family stands outside their hut. The roof is tied down and weighted against the Arctic gales.

The barren coast of Labrador

Sailing west from Erik's Fjord, Leif and his crew had no trouble in identifying their first landmark. It was clearly the coast which Bjarni had sighted. Leif anchored off the shore, then lowered a boat and landed. He was the first European on record to set foot on American soil.

The *Greenland Saga* paints a bleak picture of the new land. "There was no grass to be seen, and the **hinterland** was covered with great glaciers, and between the glaciers and the shore the land was like one great slab of rock. It seemed to them a worthless country."

Where were they? There is no way of knowing for certain, but from the description given in the *Saga* Leif and his men had probably landed on the southern tip of the barren Arctic island now known as Baffin Island. Pleased that he had done better than Bjarni and had, at least, set foot on the new land, Leif named it **Helluland**, or "Slab-Land," after its huge slabs of bare rock. They then returned to the ship and headed out to sea again, sailing on towards the south.

Soon they sighted land again and it was clear it looked like the country described by Bjarni.

"This country was flat and wooded, with white sandy beaches wherever they went, and the lands sloped gently down to the sea."

The forests of the new land provided timber for the Greenland settlements. It was little wonder that Leif gave it the name he did: **Markland**, or "Forest-Land." This was almost certainly the coast of southern Labrador.

After making only the briefest of landings on Markland, Leif headed south again, searching now for the third and last of the strange lands sighted by Bjarni.

◁ Heading inshore to make the first recorded landing by Europeans in America, Leif Eriksson steers cautiously towards the bleak and barren coast of the country first sighted by Bjarni, to which Leif gives the name of Helluland (Slab-Land). Crewmen prepare to drop anchor before the first venture ashore.

A land where vines grow

After heading out to sea from the wooded coast of Markland, Leif sailed for two days before a north-easterly wind before he sighted land again. They headed for its nearest point: an offshore island, on which they landed. The *Greenland Saga* describes the crew's reactions in moving terms:

"They went ashore and looked about them. The weather was fine. There was dew on the grass, and the first thing they did was get some of it on their hands and put it to their lips. It seemed the sweetest thing they had ever tasted! Then they went back to their ship and sailed into the sound that lay between the island and the headland jutting out to the north."

At a point "where a river flowed out of a lake," Leif decided to halt for the winter and a period of exploration. His crew set about building stone and turf houses at this base camp, knowing that at least they had one delicious food source: "There was no lack of salmon in the river or the lake, bigger salmon than they had ever seen."

To explore the new land, Leif divided his crew into two. Half was to stay at the houses, while half made journeys of exploration. He ordered that they were not to become separated, or travel so far that they could not return the same evening.

The explorers had to adjust to a new pattern of night and day, for the daylight hours in the strange new land were longer than in Greenland or Iceland. They also noticed that the nights and days were of more even length than in the northern colonies. One very important fact recorded in the *Greenland Saga* was that on the shortest day of the year the sun was already up by 9 o'clock in the morning, and did not set until after 5 o'clock in the evening. This gives a useful clue to where Leif and his men landed, because the pattern of night and day changes with the latitude north or south. With the hours mentioned, Leif's crew set up their base somewhere between Latitude 50° and Latitude 40°. This lies between the Gulf of St Lawrence and New Jersey – and salmon are not usually found south of the Hudson River.

Despite Leif's orders, there came a day when one of his crewmen, Tyrkir, was found missing. Leif sent out a search party which soon found Tyrkir – and the momentous news he brought. "I have found vines and grapes!"

Knowing that he had discovered a far wealthier land than his father had ever found, Leif ordered his crew to load a cargo consisting of grapes, and cut vines and timber with which to return to Greenland. Before sailing for home, Leif named the new land for its natural qualities – **Vinland**, or "Wine-land," after its gift of grapes.

▷ Leif's search party finds the straying Tyrkir and hears his news: the discovery of grapes which gave the new land its name of "Vinland." The *Saga* notes that Tyrkir had been born in Germany, and recognized the wild grape-vines from those he had known in his native land.

The settlers arrive

Leif Eriksson won his nickname of "Leif the Lucky" for rescuing 15 shipwrecked sailors. This was during the return to Greenland after his Vinland voyage, probably in the spring of 988.

Like Bjarni, Leif the Lucky chose never to return to Vinland. However, his brother Thorvald was eager to go, and Leif gave him his ship – the same "lucky ship" used by Bjarni. With a crew of 30 men, Thorvald sailed for Vinland in 989 or 990.

Following Leif's directions, Thorvald reached Vinland and found the huts that Leif had built, known as "Leif's Houses". They were used as a base camp during two summers that were spent exploring the Vinland coast.

Thorvald Eriksson never came home from Vinland. During the second summer, he and his men were attacked in their ship by native warriors paddling boats made from skin. The Greenlanders called them "savage wretches" or **Skraelings**. This is thought to be the first mention in history of American Indians. They were driven off by the Greenlanders' swords and axes, but not before a Skraeling arrow had given Thorvald a fatal wound. He was the first European to be buried on American soil.

Thorvald's crew spent the winter in Vinland before sailing for Greenland with a cargo of grapes and vines. When they returned they heard the news of Erik's death.

The third son of Erik the Red, Thorstein, was determined to sail to

△ Thorfinn's colonists in Vinland – a land far kinder than any they had known in the north. Their farm animals thrived on the abundant pasture, while the colonists found all the timber they needed for building and trade.

Vinland and bring home his brother's body. He sailed from Greenland with his wife Gudrid and a crew of 25, but they never reached Vinland. After many weeks at sea at the mercy of the weather, they were blown back to Greenland. Later, Thorstein and many of his crew died of disease.

However, these unlucky voyages did not discourage eager talk of "Vinland the Good", and soon there were plans for a permanent settlement to be made in the new land. The leader was Thorfinn Karlsefni, a wealthy Norwegian who arrived in Greenland the summer after Thorstein Eriksson's death. Thorfinn married Thorstein's widow Gudrid, and lived with Leif the Lucky at Brattahlid.

At some time between 998–1000 Thorfinn sailed for Vinland. This was over 500 years before the first English attempt to found a colony in America. He took with him 60 men and 5 women, and a wide range of farm animals including a bull for breeding.

Once ashore at Leif's Houses, they put the animals out to pasture. Thorfinn was shrewd and ordered timber to be cut and left to dry out. This would make useful cargo to sell in Greenland. The little colony passed a peaceful first winter in its huts.

But with the coming of spring came the Skraelings.

Battle with the Skraelings

For a while at least, there were hopes of peace between Thorfinn's people and the Skraelings. The first encounters were peaceful enough, with Skraelings approaching the settlement eager to trade furs for the milk provided by the colonists' herd of cattle.

To the Vikings from Greenland, the Skraelings seemed small and evil-looking. Their hair was coarse; they had large eyes and broad cheekbones. The colonists distrusted the Skraelings from the start, especially their keen interest in steel weapons.

Thorfinn ordered that no weapons were to be given to the Skraelings when trading. It was not long before a Skraeling, who was caught trying to steal weapons, was killed. The first attempt by the Skraelings to take what they wanted was foiled by the colonists' bull, whose angry bellowing caused the Skraelings to flee in panic. Inevitably, an armed attack soon came, forcing the Vikings to fight for their lives.

The Skraelings had the advantage of numbers, and used a "secret weapon" new to Viking warriors: a heavy throwing-stone, catapulted from the end of a pole. But this was a battle of the Iron Age – Viking swords and axes – against the Stone Age. Two Vikings were killed by Skraeling arrows and clubs to avenge the death of four Skraelings. The Skraelings fled.

Thorfinn's men saw the retreating Skraelings pick up the axe of one of the dead Vikings.

"One of them chopped at a tree with it, and then each one in turn tried it; they all thought it a wonderful find, because of its sharpness. One of them hacked at a rock with the axe, and the axe broke; and thinking it worthless now because it would not withstand stone, they threw it away."

◁ Arrows fly as the Skraelings press their attack against Thorfinn's settlers – the first recorded battle in history between the white man and the American Indian. It is possible that the Skraelings were members of the "Micmac" or the now-extinct "Beothuk" tribes. Though shaken by the novelty of the Skraelings' throwing-stones, the Vikings relied on their weapons and their trusty "shield-wall" to break the fury of the Skraelings' attack.

The end of the story

The battle with the Skraelings had ended in victory, and Thorfinn's settlers were left in peace throughout the following winter. But Thorfinn knew that there was now no hope of founding a permanent colony in Vinland. The colonists were too few in number, and they would never be able to live in peace.

In the spring after the battle, Thorfinn told his people that they must return to Greenland. "They made ready for the voyage and took with them much valuable produce: vines and grapes and furs. They went out to sea and reached Erik's Fjord safely and spent the winter there."

Next year – maybe 1003 or 1004 – Thorfinn sailed for Iceland and Norway with a ship full of produce.

So ended the most famous attempt by the Greenlanders to settle in the land discovered by Bjarni Herjolfsson and Leif Eriksson: Vinland the Good.

How trustworthy are the stories of the Vinland voyages? And if the story they tell is true, where exactly was Vinland?

Though details of the sagas were almost certainly embroidered by the storytellers of later years, there is no reason at all to doubt that these voyages could have been made. Viking seafarers were used to much longer voyages, and the distance from Greenland to North America is far shorter than that from Norway to Greenland.

Recent archaeological excavations on the island of Newfoundland have found clear traces of Viking settlement, while mentions of Vinland and Markland – Greenland's nearest source of timber – are found in Icelandic writings 100 years after Leif Eriksson's famous voyage.

The Bishop of Greenland, Erik Gnupsson, sailed for Vinland in 1121, probably with the intention of converting the Skraelings to Christianity. Last of the Vinland voyagers, he was never seen again.

▷ L'Anse aux Meadows in northern Newfoundland, where clear evidence of Viking settlement has been found. Apart from hut outlines, there are open hearths where the settlers smelted iron ore, known as "bog iron," found in the soil.

◁ As Thorfinn's ships head out to sea on their return voyage to Greenland, the Skraelings of Vinland curiously pick over the litter left behind in the abandoned settlement.

Glossary

Aegir God of the sea in Viking myth.

Althing Law-making "government" of Iceland.

Amidships The middle of a ship.

Beitass Long spar used to stiffen the sail when sailing close to the wind.

Bulwarks The sides of a ship above the water-line.

Clinker-built Ship or boat built from overlapping planks.

▽ The Viking sea route "west over seas" from Norway, via the Faroes and Iceland to Greenland. Voyages from Greenland to North America were far shorter than those from Norway to Greenland.

Drekar "Dragon" – favorite name for a Viking warship.

Eastern Settlement Erik the Red's main Greenland colony (modern Julianehäb).

Fjord Long, narrow sea inlet which runs between high banks or cliffs.

Greenland Saga A medieval Icelandic saga which tells of the discovery of Vinland by the Vikings.

Helluland "Slab-Land" (probably Baffin Island).

Hinterland Area behind the land lying along the coast.

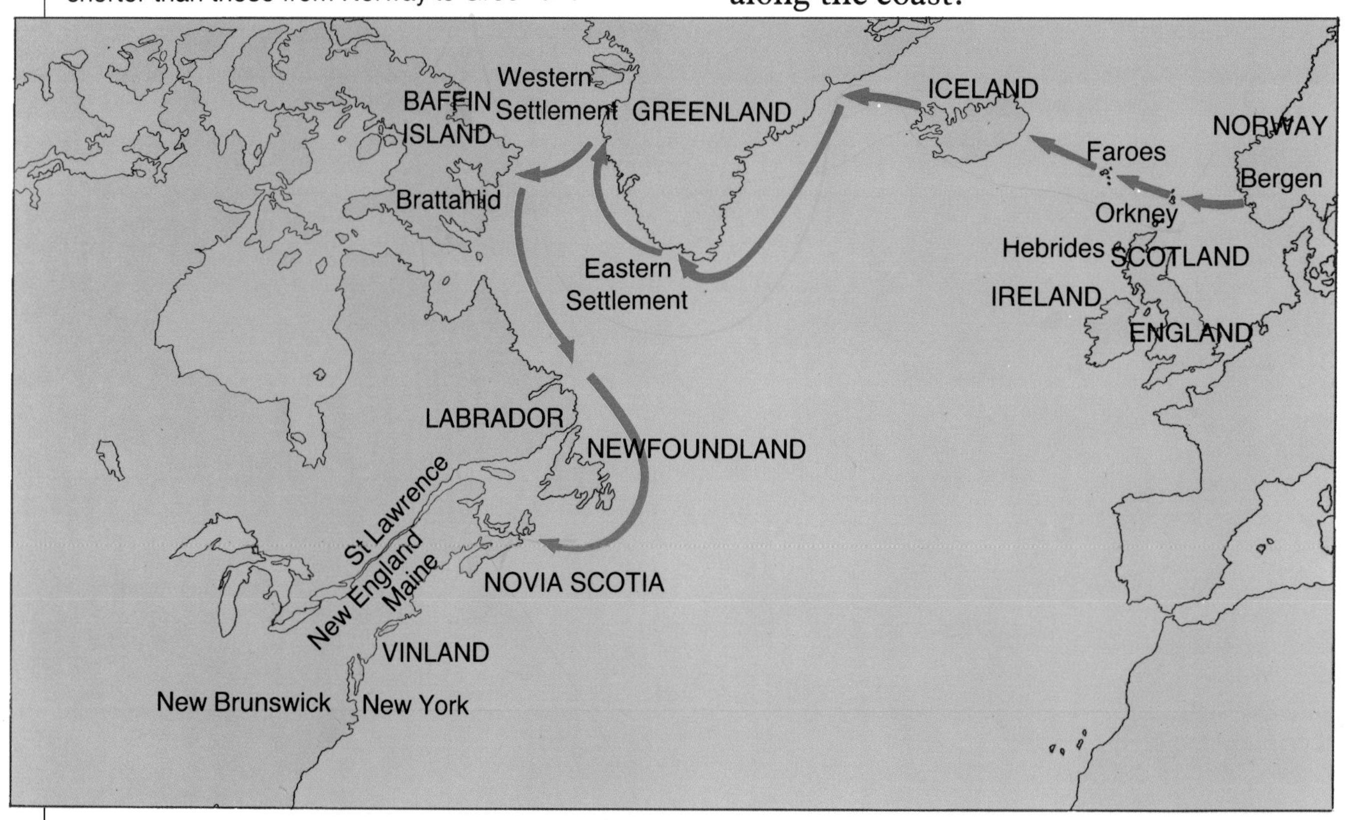

Timechart

Knorr Cargo ship used by Viking merchants and settlers.

Markland "Forest Land" (probably Labrador).

Narwhal Small Arctic whale, prized by Viking hunters for its spiral projecting tooth that looks like a unicorn's horn.

Pelorus "Sun compass." Hand-held bearing dial used in navigation for estimating position by sighting the altitude of the sun or stars.

Saga Norwegian or Icelandic heroic account of legends and histories.

Skraelings "Savage wretches" – name given by the first Viking settlers of Vinland to the native warriors.

Starboard The right or "steering-board" side of a ship, where the steering-oar was mounted.

Step Heavy timber above a ship's keel, supporting the mast.

Vinland "Wine-Land" – the name given by Leif Eriksson to the land he found south-west of Greenland, where grapevines grew.

Western Settlement The second Viking colony in Greenland (modern Godthaab).

c. 789AD First recorded Viking raid on England.
c. 793 Vikings raid Iona in Scotland.
c. 825 Vikings settle on Faroe Islands.
c. 860 First Vikings sight Iceland.
c. 890 Ingolf Arnarsson begins settlement of Iceland.
c. 900 Gunnbjörn Ulfsson sights Greenland.
c. 981 Erik explores Greenland.
c. 983 Erik the Red returns to Iceland.
c. 986 Erik begins settlement of Greenland.
c. 986 Bjarni Herjolfsson sights land to the west and south of Greenland.
c. 987 Leif Eriksson lands in Helluland and Markland and spends the winter in Vinland.
c. 989 Leif's brother, Thorvald, sails to Vinland.
c. 992 Thorvald dies from an arrow-wound when attacked by Skraelings.
c. 1000–1003 Thorfinn Karlsefni's attempt to settle in Vinland.
1121 Bishop Erik Gnupsson of Greenland sails for Vinland. He is never heard of again.
1261–62 Greenland and Iceland come under Norwegian rule.
1410 Last ship from Greenland reaches Iceland.
1492 Christopher Columbus re-discovers America.
c. 1500 Last Greenland colonists die out.

Index